Snuggle Sessions

with God

by
Alisha Ritchie

Snuggle Sessions with God

Alisha Ritchie

Alisha Ritchie ©2017
All rights reserved
ISBN 13:9780998833903
ISBN 10:0998833908

DWB PUBLISHING
www.dancingwithbearpublishing.com

Snuggle Sessions with God   Alisha Ritchie

Foreword

I remember when my children were little—sometimes it seems like just yesterday and other times if feels like a million years ago. One of the best things about being a mom is getting to snuggle with them. They would love to crawl onto my lap and we would cuddle underneath a blanket while reading one of their favorite books. Every night, we would pile into their beds and say our prayers together. During those times, we snuggled, hugged, even rough—housed a little, but we were always physically close to each other. It is undeniable that we felt close to each other emotionally as well. These special times were our "snuggle sessions. Some of the sweetest and best memories we have shared have been during those close times together. The other day I heard a song that reminded me of some of those sweet memories. The song's message spoke of how God wants nothing more than to have us close to Him. There's a lot of truth to that song. As a parent, I want to be close to my children. Whether I am snuggling with them when they are two years-old or as teenagers, I want nothing more than to have a close relationship with them.

God feels the same way about His children. He wants to have "snuggle sessions" with us and desires to have a close, personal relationship. He wants to be the one to comfort us when things go wrong, wrapping His tender arms around us. God also wants to be close to share the joys and triumphs we have on those mountain tops of life. It really makes sense that as my Heavenly Father, He longs for my love and attention, just as my children do of me.

I have been inspired to deepen my relationship with God, drawing closer to Him as I have written this book. It doesn't matter how old I am or how long I've been a Christian, God still values me and the relationship we share as Father and child. Just as I remember all those times of bonding with my kids, I believe God remembers our close times together too. I want to continue to share more of those intimate times with Him as I learn more about who He is and the love He offers. And it is my hope that you, too, will grow in your faith as you share your very own "snuggle sessions with God" while reading this book.

Happy reading and blessings to you!

~ One ~
Shaky Sand

For God has already placed Jesus Christ as the one and only
foundation, and no other foundation can be laid.
—1 Corinthians 3:11 GNT

I remember my first trip to the beach like it was yesterday. My parents have never been "beach" people and we often vacationed in the mountains. So naturally, my first experience with the coast was very memorable.

I traveled with a family friend to the North Carolina shore when I was in fourth grade. We didn't get to stay in an ocean front house but were only one street over, well within walking distance. Once we had unpacked our clothes, we excitedly changed into our swim suits, grabbed a towel, and headed out for my first experience with the ocean.

As I stood in the sand, near the breaking waves, I was mesmerized by the peaceful lull of the crashing waves onto shore. Water stretched out before me as far as I could see, the sun shimmering on the waves as they billowed and rolled. The smell of salt overtook my senses as the gentle breeze swirled my hair.

I was tempted to go closer...

I gradually crept to the water, standing just within reach for the ocean to meet my feet. The cool water splashed my toes and then was pulled rhythmically back into the big sea.

Suddenly, I was overtaken by fear, as the sand sifted from beneath my feet. The grains of sand were shaky, being pulled right out from underneath me,   definitely not to be trusted. The sensations fooled me as I perceived I was drifting into the water, unstable, unsafe.

Almost losing my balance, I inched away from the waves to the safety of dry sand. I needed to be where I felt secure, where the ground was solid beneath my feet. I needed a firm foundation.

My first experience at the beach reminds me of the many times as an adult I still feel like I'm standing on shaky sand.

Mistakes, failed relationships, poor attitudes, and just the busyness of life, can make me feel insecure. But the Bible reminds me in 1 Corinthians I shouldn't fear when my world is plagued by shifting sand underfoot.

Jesus Christ is my true foundation, my rock. He is the only reason for my existence and provides unwavering security, even when everything seems out of control. He will never let me down, as He is the foundation of eternal peace and life.

Put your trust in Jesus today by releasing your problems to Him through prayer. Be comforted as the waves of peace roll over you, never being shaken from your firm foundation in God's son and His love.

"Heavenly Father, thank you for the blessings You have given me. Make my foundation firm in You, even when it seems like everything else is falling apart around me. Grant me peace in the security of Your never ending love and protection. In Jesus' name I pray, Amen."

Your thoughts:

_____

_____

_____

_____

_____

_____

_____

_____

_____

_____

~ Two ~
Welcome Home

"Create in me a clean heart, O God, and renew a steadfast spirit within me."
—Psalm 51:10 NIV

"Company's coming. Quick, get the vacuum cleaner!" I yell to my husband who's lounging in the recliner.

Our friends just phoned to say they would arrive at our house in a half-hour.

Thirty minutes? That's not enough time to get this house in order, I worried.

Quickly I enlist the help of my husband and two children to make a mad dash at disguising our house as presentable. We pick up clutter that litters our den. Carpets are vacuumed, floors swept, and dirty towels that to seem to multiply overnight on the bathroom floor are tossed in the hamper. Amazingly the tasks are completed just in the nick of time to welcome our friends into our home.

I wonder if the Holy Spirit ever feels the home of my heart is untidy? Do I work to keep my heart clean and pure for Him? After all, there are no surprise visits—as a believer, He is always there as an inhabitant. Unfortunately, sin finds a way to creep in my home and make a mess. If I'm not careful, things can get out of control very quickly, just like in my earthly house.

In Psalm the Bible tells us, "Create in me a clean heart, O God, and renew a steadfast spirit within me." The key verse reminds me that I am called to repentance to foster a clean heart for the Holy Spirit. The beauty of repentance is that I really don't have much work to do on my own. God takes care of the messy sin that invades the home of my heart. I only need to sincerely ask for forgiveness and turn away from my sin.

God will revitalize His spirit within us. The sacrifice of Jesus acts like a cleaning service or maid for my soul. By the blood shed for me on the cross, my sins can be forgiven and my heart can be made sparkling fresh again.

Resolve that you will not roll out the welcome mat for sin into the home of your heart. Be selective in the visitors you allow in your home. Pray that God will point out clutter that needs to be eliminated and sincerely repent. Express your thankfulness and praise to the Lord for His sacrifice of Jesus, enabling us to have hearts that are once again pure and glorifying to Him.

Your thoughts:

_____

_____

_____

_____

_____

_____

_____

_____

_____

_____

_____

_____

_____

_____

_____

~ Three ~
Etch-A-Sketch Heart

But if we walk in the light, as He is in the light, we have fellowship with one another, and the blood of Jesus, His Son, purifies us from all sin.
—1 John 1:7 NIV

The cutest four-year-old girl in the world beckoned me to play with her on the floor of her bedroom. She's artistic and imaginative so naturally she's interested in the Etch-A-Sketch®. We sat cross-legged together on her fluffy, teal rug as she demonstrated her artistic talents with the toy.

She made swirls and patterns and then formed a perfect heart over her creation. Bored with what I consider creative genius, my daughter gave the toy a couple of mighty shakes, erasing her efforts.

"Why did you erase it?"

"I didn't like it. It had all that stuff in it. It looked messy and I want to make a new one," she replied.

She didn't like her messy heart. Suddenly I realized I felt that way about my own heart at times, too. I try to do the "right" things by attending church services, reading the Bible and teaching a Sunday School class. My children are taught the importance of morals, good values, and to treat people with dignity and respect.

But I'm not perfect. Sin invades me because I am human and my heart continues to get messy. There is no hope for me to create a new, clean heart on my own—only my Savior can make me new.

The Bible teaches that our hearts are purified by the sacrifice of Jesus on the cross. No matter how dirty and ugly our souls get, His blood is powerful enough to make it pure. Jesus conquered death to ensure we would have **life** through Him. His gift to us makes our hearts clean just as the little girl desired her decorative heart to be.

> *Lord, thank you for the death of Your Son on the cross. Thank you for the gift of salvation and forgiveness. Help me to live in a way that brings honor and glory to You. In Jesus's name, Amen.*

Your thoughts:

_____

_____

_____

_____

_____

_____

_____

_____

_____

_____

_____

_____

_____

~ Four ~

Dad's Grace

For sin shall no longer be your master, because you are not under the law, but under grace.
—Romans 6:19 NIV

In seventh grade I made a terrible mistake. Trying to fit in with my peers, I made a choice to smoke cigarettes with some friends at the mall. Of course, I ended up getting caught and was scared of how my parents would react to my foolish behavior.

I don't remember a lot of the details but one thing sticks out clearly in my mind—Dad's reaction to my mistake. While sitting on the edge of my bed, he said, "Alisha, if this is the worst thing you ever do, I think we'll be okay."

I have always remembered his words. In that moment when he should have yelled or berated me, he chose to give me grace. My father knew how horrible I felt and chose to offer me unmerited forgiveness instead of harsh words.

Along life's way I have made even more mistakes—some worse than others. But the one constant is my dad's shower of grace upon me. He demonstrates my Heavenly Father's love and grace by his actions toward me.

In Romans we are reminded that as born-again believers in Jesus Christ, we are no longer subject to the law. Sin no longer has a hold on us because of the grace God provided by sacrificing His Son. As the verse implies, we are under His protection of grace. He has freely given it to us even though we do not deserve it.

When we mess up, God is not waiting to judge us and rebuke us for our bad behavior. He is there to talk with us on the edge of our beds, like my dad, sharing His mercy and love with us. He knows we experience failure in our lives. We disappoint Him with our words, thoughts, actions and sin too many times to fathom. But His grace is everlasting, always seeking to find us in our times of despair. He puts no limit on the amount of times we can come to Him for mercy. God wants us to realize our weakness and humbly petition Him for help. For certain, He will not disappoint us.

Are there areas in your life that you need to seek God's forgiveness and grace? Pray to God for help in those situations and find peace in knowing His mercy is unceasing. Sit on the edge of your bed and talk with God, expectant of His wonderful, abounding love and grace.

Your thoughts:

_____

_____

_____

_____

_____

_____

_____

_____

_____

_____

_____

_____

_____

_____

_____

~ Five~
Refrigerator Envy

So in Christ Jesus you are all children of God through faith.
—Galatians 3:26 NIV

My refrigerator is a hot mess. I love to display my two children's latest photographs as well as some of their baby photos. Hung on the corner of the fridge is a lovely drawing of a cross on a hill my sweet Abby created when she was nine. I also have a magnet Zack made for me when he was a preschooler.

Scripture verses and inspirational quotes decorate the white metal appliance, hopefully giving our family encouragement. My refrigerator displays a wide variety of stuff but it all relates to my precious family. I absolutely love it. But I will admit that sometimes I look at the fridge and think, "What a mess!"

I'm envious of people who own the perfect fridge. You know, the kind of appliance that could be in a magazine ad. Perpetually clean and sparkling, the clutter is minimum, pictures are neatly blocked and are sometimes arranged in chronological order. I have always wanted to have a refrigerator like this but have been unable to achieve it. I just can't bring myself to pack away those memories and pieces of my heart that hang there.

I recently questioned, *I wonder what God's refrigerator in Heaven looks like? Does He have my photo hanging on it to remind Him of the day I surrendered my heart to Him? Or does He put little Scripture verse notes up there that apply specifically to me because He wants to give me inspiration throughout my day?*

The Bible states in Galatians, "So in Christ Jesus you are all children of God through faith". God has a lot of adopted children because we have accepted Jesus as our personal Lord and Savior through faith. As believers, we claim inheritance in Heaven as God's children. He loves each of us dearly and no doubt is proud of us, like any Father of is children.

I imagine God's refrigerator resembles mine—cluttered and messy but with memorabilia, accomplishments and achievements of His family. We are loved and His fridge shows it.

Be uplifted that God unselfishly lavishes His beautiful love on you as His son or daughter. Gain inspiration today to become a member of God's family if you are not already His child. Surrender your life to Him today. You don't want to miss out on having your photo displayed on the King's refrigerator in Heaven.

Your thoughts:

_____

_____

_____

_____

_____

_____

_____

_____

_____

_____

_____

_____

_____

_____

~ Six~
Tent Dweller

I long to dwell in your tent forever...
—Psalm 61:4 NIV

In Nehemiah from the Bible, the seven-day Festival of the Tabernacles is referenced. During this event, the Israelites lived in temporary tents or shelters they made from tree branches and twigs. This special celebration served as a reminder of how God rescued them from slavery in Egypt and protected them while wandering in the desert.

No doubt, as they remembered and celebrated, the Israelites were filled with joy and gratitude for all they had been blessed them with. They listened to His Word. The people stopped their everyday routines and focused on God, praising Him for His provision and care.

Today's key verse prompts me to think of how I yearn to dwell in God's tent of protection forever. I want to stay in the safety of His shelter, away from life's problems and obstacles. God's everlasting strength, love and sanctuary are surely things I cannot survive without.

"I long to dwell in your tent forever..."

But more importantly, I want to dwell in His tent so I am completely focused on Him, as the Israelites were. I desire to remember all the times God has guarded me from harm and recall the countless prayers He has answered on my behalf. I want to remember everything about my walk with Him.

In His shelter, peace finds me. It thwarts away the distractions of life that threaten to pull me away from honoring and praising the Lord.

"I long to dwell in your tent forever..."

"Lord, help me seek shelter in Your tent of protection. Guide me to always remember Your blessings. Create in me a thankful heart, giving honor and praise to You forever. In Jesus' name, Amen."

Your thoughts:

_____

_____

_____

_____

_____

_____

_____

_____

_____

_____

_____

_____

_____

_____

_____

_____

_____

_____

_____

~ Seven~
Boone Blizzard

"And we know that God causes all things to work together for good to those who love God, to those who are called according to His purpose."
Romans 8:28 NASB

The SUV was loaded down with my family's snow gear, snacks, and supplies, all in readiness for our fun-filled weekend in the mountains of Boone, North Carolina. Who cares if the weather man forecasted a mini blizzard? We wouldn't let that stop our fun of snow tubing.

Then reality sat in. The closer we got to Boone, the more snow we saw. The whole world was covered in a blanket of white. The roads were dangerous, especially for an SUV without four—wheel drive. We sat tight-lipped, mindful of what could happen as my husband navigated our vehicle along the winding road. Everything went well, that is, until we encountered *it,* a monster of a hill blocking passage to refuge, our hotel on the other side.

We couldn't get enough tire traction to make it up the steep hill and slid backwards and sideways, each time getting dangerously close to the traffic-filled road behind us. Finally admitting defeat, my family and I parked the SUV at the base of the hill, grabbed our luggage and trudged in the snow and freezing temperature up the mountain to our hotel. This was definitely not how I wanted our quality family time weekend to start.

And it only got worse from there. Nothing turned out as we had planned. I lost my favorite scarf, my daughter got an awful stomach virus, and we had to cancel our tubing adventure. We felt helpless and hopeless.

Maybe you have experienced times like this in your life. There are days when nothing seems to go right and you don't know how to make it better. Find hope in the One who is in control of everything—the ever-present, ever-steady Lord. When your world is turned upside down and you are dizzy from trying to focus on anything that makes sense, rely on God to help you through.

Seek comfort in the words from the book of Romans: *And we know that God causes all things to work together for good to those who love God, to those who are called according to His purpose.*

Even when our perfectly laid-out plans fail, God is in control. We can trust God at His word that He ultimately has our best interests at heart and has good things in store for us. It may be hard to see at the time, but eventually all things will work for good according to His will.

Our family trip to Boone was a teachable experience. We learned a valuable lesson about never purchasing an SUV without four-wheel drive. Rather than allowing our ruined plans to spoil our trip, we discovered alternatives such as a wonderful gem mining place that proved to be a lot of fun. And most importantly, we made memories that will definitely last a lifetime, which was our goal in the first place.

Let God help you discover the silver linings in those difficult circumstances that befall you.

Your thoughts:

_____

_____

_____

_____

_____

_____

_____

_____

_____

~ Eight~
Duct Taped Stool

Jesus replied: 'Love the Lord your God with all your heart and with all your soul and with all your mind.' Matthew 22:37 NIV

He was a little rough around the edges. He wore mismatched clothes and sported disheveled hair. His thick country accent made him hard to understand at times but I loved my new physical therapy patient. He had a heart of gold that shone with his dynamic personality.

We undertook therapy underneath in an old shed because his house was inaccessible to me because of his vicious guard dog. Every day we worked on exercises to help him become stronger and walk better, and every day he offered me the same thing—an old duct taped stool to sit on. It was clearly the better of the two stools in his possession. The other stool was more tattered and faded, with uneven legs to lend it to wobble. He always sacrificed the better stool to me—the piece of furniture with more cushion and even legs. It doesn't seem like much but it is the best he had and freely gave.

Through my patient's character, I am reminded of what the Bible says about giving God my best. In Matthew, we learn that we are to love God with all of our heart, soul, and mind. In other words, we give God everything, our very best. We may feel unworthy of the gifts we have to bestow on our Savior but we are called to give what we do have.

By wholeheartedly serving others, we are giving our best. And using the talents we have been blessed with to worship Him, we are giving the greatest part of ourselves. When we rely on courage from God to point others to Jesus, we are following His will for our lives.

Be encouraged to give God your best today just as my patient gave me his very best. God craves all that you have to offer Him so that you can enter into a deeper personal relationship with Him.

Your thoughts:

_____

_____

_____

_____

_____

_____

_____

_____

_____

_____

_____

_____

_____

_____

_____

_____

_____

_____

~ Nine~
Hearing Impaired

Listen and hear my voice; pay attention to what I say.
Isaiah 28:23 NIV

For as long as I can remember, my mom has always had a hearing impairment. It was so debilitating that she got a hearing aid many years ago. While the aid is very helpful, it also has its downfalls. For instance, when mom is in a large crowd with people talking, she struggles. Loud noise is overwhelming. The hearing aid cannot distinguish between sounds and just makes EVERYTHING deafening. Frustrated, Mom elects to turn her aid off in situations like this and bask in the calmness of peace and quiet. There are times in my life when I wish I could turn off the background noise. All the voices of the world are a distraction, keeping me from completely being in tune to listening to God.

The key verse from the book of Isaiah inspires me: *Listen and hear my voice; pay attention to what I say.* A small verse that provides a powerful reminder to constantly seek to hear God's voice in my boisterous world. God specifically tells us to listen and hear in this verse. While both words are verbs, they also imply that we not only perceive God's voice but take it into consideration, concentrate on it, take notice while acting on it.

Be encouraged today as God wants you to hear His voice. He is constantly communicating and desires to be in continuous fellowship with you. Pray for guidance on ways to tune out the bombarding chatter of society and focus on the voice of the only One who truly matters.

Your thoughts:

_____

_____

_____
_____
_____
_____
_____
_____
_____
_____
_____
_____
_____
_____
_____
_____
_____
_____
_____
_____
_____
_____
_____
_____
_____
_____
_____

~Ten~

Sassy Fox

Be still, and know that I am God...   Psalm 46:10 ESV

My cat Sherbet (named because of his orange Dreamsicle™ coloring and called Sherby for short) looks like a sassy fox. Literally...he has the bushiest tail I've ever seen. He is a stunningly beautiful cat. His long, thick fur promotes a plump stature with his golden eyes sparkling as they coordinate with his soft coat.

Sherby has been a member of our family for over two years. He has definitely made our lives more interesting because of his curious nature and restless spirit that always seems to get him in trouble. There have been numerous times that Sherby has explored an area that he has no business investigating. He once roamed underneath our house only to be trapped for hours, and another time napped the night away in our SUV (outfitted with leather seats). Most recently, he climbed to the top of a huge tree only to discover that he didn't know how to come down.

I am reminded that I too have a restless spirit. It is difficult for me to slow down long enough to enjoy God's beauty or His gentle whispers. The Bible tells us in Psalm, "Be still, and know that I am God."

Perhaps you really need to hear those powerful words. Stop rushing around like a whirlwind. Cultivate a spirit that is satisfied in this season of life-right where you are now. Let God show you His complete peace and satisfaction by spending time abiding in Him. Be refreshed in knowing that you don't have to wander, explore, or search. He is already there waiting for you—waiting for you to be still and know that He is God.

Heavenly Father, you know

*my heart, my soul, my mind.
You know every single need
that I have. You alone can
help to calm my restless spirit.
Show me how to find ways to
slow the pace in my life that I
may better know you. Thank
you for the blessings of my life
and my opportunity to spend
time with you. In Jesus' name,
Amen.*

Your thoughts:

_____

_____

_____

_____

_____

_____

_____

_____

_____

_____

_____

_____

~Eleven~

Twenty-three Pounds

"For I am the Lord your God who takes hold of your right hand and says to you, Do not fear; I will help you."
Isaiah 41:13 NIV

Twenty-three pounds. That's exactly how much my son Zack's backpack weighs. It is stuffed with enough books and school supplies for six middle school classes. He has a locker but chooses to carry all this weight around with him every day...all day. Zack doesn't feel he has time to get to his locker between classes or maybe he is partly just lazy. The point is that he carries a tremendous burden on his back by his own choice.

As his mom, this frustrates me because I know it is not good to carry this heavy load all the time. And I can only imagine how tiring this must be.

But then I am prompted to think, *Isn't this how I act too? Don't I carry around so many burdens by my own choice?*

Sometimes I am reluctant to give all my worries to the Lord. The Scriptures remind us that God is here to help. He is beside us, going through what we are experiencing. God desires to give us encouragement and hope in our times of need.

Release your burdens to Him so that He can lighten your load. If we get rid of the stuff that is weighing us down in our backpacks of life, we have so much more room for the wonderful things that God has in store for us. God wants to shower us with blessings of peace, love, contentment, and joy. We just need to make sure we make enough room to receive them.

Your thoughts:

_____

_____

_____

_____

_____

_____

_____

_____

_____

_____

_____

_____

_____

_____

_____

_____

_____

_____

_____

_____

_____

_____

_____

_____

_____

_____

~Twelve~

God Makes a Way

Forget the former things; do not dwell on the past. See, I am doing a new thing! Now it springs up; do you not perceive it? I am making a way in the wilderness and streams in the waste.
Isaiah 43: 18-19 NIV

I noticed the house right away as I drove by. It was hard not to notice a yard filled with a wide gamut of clutter: car parts; tools; furniture; toys and trash.

The house wasn't in much better shape. However, amidst all the mess, I noticed a small handmade sign staked in the yard that read "God makes a way." In the depth of all the clutter and disarray, I focused on one item—the sign.

My heart is touched as I think about what the words on the sign truly meant. Life often gets jumbled with a hectic schedule, relationship demands, my to-do list, and even sin. However, God forges a way and directs my steps.

The Lord tells us in Isaiah, "Forget the former things; do not dwell on the past. See, I am doing a new thing! Now it springs up; do you not perceive it? I am making a way in the wilderness and streams in the wasteland."

These scriptures are a reminder to not dwell on our past and have faith that God will help us make it through the trials of life. Sometimes we cannot gain enough focus because of the jumbled mess that creeps into our lives. We lose our compass for direction and wonder *Where we should go from here?*

Find comfort in knowing that no matter how hopeless your situation seems, God is there to make a way through the mess. Pray for renewed trust to navigate through your cluttered life and help you find refuge in His love and direction. Keep your mind's eye focused on the yard sign that reads "God makes a way."

Your thoughts:

_____

_____

_____

_____

_____

_____

_____

_____

_____

_____

_____

_____

_____

_____

_____

_____

_____

_____

_____

_____

_____

_____

~Thirteen~

Sleepless Hotel Nights

And He said to them, 'Go into all the world and proclaim the gospel to the whole creation.
Mark 16:15 ESV

I laid in the dark in a strange hotel room. I knew I should sleep (we had a big day ahead of us at a theme park), but my mind continued to wander.

How many people have laid in this same bed or used the TV remote? How many others have pulled out the Bible from the desk drawer to read? It amazes me to think of the many individuals and families that have stayed in this exact hotel room.

People from all different walks of life have been exactly where I am tonight. No doubt some of those people were from other countries. Surely some of those people were happy and some were sad. No doubt some of those people needed Jesus.

Those random thoughts prompted me to remember Scripture from Mark reminding us of the great commission—go everywhere and tell others about Jesus.

Tell people about your personal encounter with Jesus Christ and the hope you have now through Him. Be a witness for Him in the way you live your life from day to day and even on those special occasions when you travel on vacation with your family. There are so many people who still need to hear the Good News. Live your life in a way that points others to Jesus. You could possibly be the only Jesus they may ever see.

The people who have stayed in this same hotel room were here only temporarily, whether for business or pleasure. However, wouldn't it be wonderful if those same people assuredly would have a permanent home in Heaven with you and me? The only way to encourage this is by sharing the Gospel with others. With God's help, you can make a difference for the Kingdom of God.

Lord, thank you for the loving me so much that I get to spend eternity in Heaven with You. Help me work diligently to share Your message of love and hope with others so that Your kingdom may be built up. In Jesus' name I pray, Amen.

Your thoughts:

_____

_____

_____

_____

_____

_____

_____

_____

_____

_____

_____

_____

_____

_____

_____

_____

~Fourteen~

Word Switcheroo

The Lord bless you and keep you; the Lord make His face shine on you and be gracious to you; the Lord turn His face toward you and give you peace. Numbers 6:24-26 NIV

As followers of Christ, the Lord wishes to bless us abundantly. He desires each moment of our lives (whether perceived as blessing or difficulty) be punctuated with thankfulness. Thus, blessings are all about perspective. What one person takes for granted and considers a nuisance is a significant blessing to another.

With God's help we can dramatically change the way we view our circumstances and world around us. By simply switching one word in our internal thinking, we gain a whole new perspective on life and all that we've been given.

For example, recently I was weary from driving my kids to and from school and their daily extra-curricular activities. I complained to my husband about the afternoon schedule saying, "I **must** drive Abby to volleyball practice and then rush to pick up Zack from driver's ed."

But by shifting one word, my new thought is, "I **get** to drive Abby to volleyball practice and then **get** to pick up Zack from Driver's Ed." My attitude transforms from bitterness to gratitude by substituting **get** for **have** in my thoughts and words. My whole viewpoint towards my children changes as the Lord reminds me of the true blessing they are to me.

I am inspired to relish having children with whom I am so involved in their daily lives. Instead of dreading this activity, I am prompted to cherish our limited time together. Those car rides have provided needed time for some wonderful conversations and memories that we'll always cherish. Any time spent with my children is never wasted—all too soon, those chauffeur sessions will come to an end.

Any circumstance, relationship, or even duty, can be a blessing if you rely on God to open your eyes to His perspective. Pray the Lord will help you perceive all things as blessings, giving thanks for His abundant grace and love He shines upon you. Seek positivity in seemingly negative situations and respond with thanksgiving when your outlook completely changes. Practice the word switcheroo and be amazed at the blessings that abound.

Your thoughts:

_____

_____

_____

_____

_____

_____

_____

_____

_____

_____

_____

_____

_____

_____

_____

_____

~Fifteen~

Flash

"He heals the brokenhearted and bandages their wounds."
Psalm 147:3 NLT

I looked at my husband's right temple in horror. The incision was much bigger than either of us had expected. I was so thankful the surgeon was able to remove all the skin cancer but knew my husband was so disappointed with being left with such a huge gash near his eyebrow.

What's more, the repair work done to his skin left him with a zig-zagged wound which resembled a lightning bolt. Thus, my kids and I affectionately nicknamed him "Flash" which he surprisingly took a liking to.

The nurse gave me wound care instructions to insure proper healing. She warned that he may develop a black eye or may have significant swelling causing it to shut completely. Ice and Tylenol™ would definitely be my husband's best friend for the next couple of days.

The healing process was going to take longer than we had anticipated. We knew that in time, the incision would heal and probably only leave a minimal scar. But it was going to take time and we were both impatient. Secretly, I wished I could magically heal the wound on my husband's face, preventing him from having to go through pain. I wanted to take the mark from him, making it better quickly.

Even though I couldn't heal his wound immediately, there is One who can heal all wounds. Scripture from Psalm reminds me that God cares deeply about His children, so much so that He tends to our wounds. I know from first-hand experience that wound care is messy work. It is not for the weak-hearted and requires multitudes of patience, diligence, and compassion.

Furthermore, wounds come in many different forms such as a broken heart, a failed relationship, or sickness. God cares about all those who are broken, for whatever reason it may be. He alone brings healing to each of those situations, giving complete peace and resolution.

> *Lord, I place my wounds in the care of*
> *You, the true Healer. Help me saturate*
> *my injuries with Your words from the Bible*
> *to promote healing in my life. Give me faith*
> *You will give the care required, as only You*
> *can do. In Jesus' name, Amen.*

Your thoughts:

_____

_____

_____

_____

_____

_____

_____

_____

_____

_____

_____

_____

~Sixteen~

Race Runner

"Therefore, since we are surrounded by such a huge crowd of witnesses to the life of faith, let us strip off every weight that slows us down, especially the sin that so easily trips us up. And let us run with endurance the race that God has set before us."
Hebrews 12:1 NLT

"Running is addictive," several of my friends assure. I always smile and nod in agreement although I totally don't get it. I want to love to run. I adore the cute shoes and sporty running outfits. I want to feel carefree as I trot down the road with the wind blowing my hair. The 5K and marathon themed races look so fun and exciting. Most of all, I crave the strength and endurance that encompasses running.

I tried sprinting with friends in the past and have taken running classes. Now my daughter has volunteered to be my running partner. We jog together on our road and she pushes me to increase my endurance, test my limits. My heart races and my breathing labors. I sweat profusely and my leg muscles ache. Honestly, running is a lot of hard work—it does not come naturally to me. But I keep trying because eventually I will get the wanted results.

My running career sparks the memory of a verse from Hebrews, "Therefore, since we are surrounded by such a huge crowd of witnesses to the life of faith, let us strip off every weight that slows us down, especially the sin that so easily trips us up. And let us run with endurance the race that God has set before us."

God tells us that the race of life will not be easy. It involves strenuous work. There will be obstacles or sin that cause us to stumble along the way. But He also gives us encouragement to keep going with perseverance. Do not give up. Keep focused on the task of doing God's will as it is laid out before you. Be inspired to do your very best today in the race in which you are participating. Maybe God is calling you to turn over sin in your life to Him. Let Him carry the burden so that excess weight doesn't prohibit your performance.

So for now, I'm running the race on my street and the race of life that God has set before me. Both are difficult at times, but both also greatly rewarding. I am still waiting for running to become an addiction, but who knows? Anything is possible with God.

Your thoughts:

_____

_____

_____

_____

_____

_____

_____

_____

_____

_____

_____

_____

_____

~Seventeen~

You're Invited

Yet to all who did receive him, to those who believed in his name, he gave the right to become children of God...
John 1:12 NIV

Don't you just love to get a pretty invitation in the mail? Gorgeous stationery makes me happy. We get a variety of invitations to weddings, baby showers, birthday parties, and graduations. I love to see the creative designs, layouts and color schemes, whether it's handmade or professional. We have received many beautiful pieces over the years which classify as works of art.

When it's time to send an invitation on behalf of my family, I get excited as my creative juices start flowing. I especially love designing stationery for my daughter's social events. Recently she hosted a *Duck Dynasty* themed party. Who would have guessed that camouflage invitations could turn out so adorable?

However, the most beautiful invitation I received was not delivered by the postal service. It was an invitation of my heart. In second grade, during revival service at church, I was invited to follow Jesus by surrendering my heart to Him. I accepted that invitation, becoming an everlasting member of God's family. Without a doubt, my acceptance of His gift was the greatest decision of my life.

The next time you go to the mail box and open up a festive card, remember God's special invitation. You too can have everlasting life with Jesus and know peace through Him. Today's verse from the Bible tells us, "Yet to all who did receive him, to those who believed in his name, he gave the right to become children of God." God extends His invitation to everyone who believes in His name. You can have a personal relationship with the One who desires to be your best friend. All other invitations pale in comparison.

> *Dear Heavenly Father, we thank you for sending your Son, Jesus, to die on the cross for us. We are humbled that you extend your invitation for eternal life to us, unworthy sinners. Please forgive us when we fail you and give us strength to share our stories with others, that more may come to know you personally. In Jesus' name we pray, Amen.*

Your thoughts:

_____

_____

_____

_____

_____

_____

_____

_____

_____

_____

_____

_____

_____

_____

~Eighteen~

Hope for the Heart

The Lord your God is in your midst, a Mighty One who will save;
He will rejoice over you with gladness; He will quiet you by His
love; He will exult over you with loud singing.
Zephaniah 3:17 ESV

I looked outside my kitchen window to see thick clouds filling the sky. Rain splattered on the deck and the gusty wind blew the barren limbs on the trees in my back yard. The view would appear cold and lonely to most people. It should seem like a gloomy, depressing day to me. I should long for the day before—it was beautiful with bright sunny skies and warmer temperatures. But actually, it looks so much brighter today than yesterday.

The previous day had been filled with one problem after another. Issues arose with my son's attitude and later I doubted the way I handled the situation. I received news that a former patient was very sick and probably only had days to live. Trouble seemed to find me at every corner and only seemed to get worse as the day went on. The sun and air were light but my heart felt heavy. The day was dark and unwelcomed even though the weather beckoned otherwise.

I am reminded of a wonderful verse in Zephaniah saying, "The Lord your God is in your midst, a Mighty One who will save; He will rejoice over you with gladness, He will quiet you by His love, He will exult over you with loud singing."

The words speak to me as I am reassured God is constantly with me and wants to rescue me from troubles and despair. He quiets my screaming, hurting heart with His wonderful love and compassion. He rejoices over me, causing me to be joyous, as I am aware of being in His awesome presence. God gives hope I will overcome my present troubles by leaning on Him and letting Him pour His gladness over my soul. He aspires me to possess a bright, sunny heart even when the storm of life is raging and begging to fill me with burdens.

Allow God to make your heart joyous, no matter what circumstance befalls you. Let God help you see hope, as He did for me, even on the gloomy days of life. Relish in knowing the Mighty One is persistently with you, helping you overcome your troubles. He is the only who can provide lasting joy for your tender soul.

Your thoughts:

_____

_____

_____

_____

_____

_____

_____

_____

_____

_____

_____

_____

_____

_____

~Nineteen~

Greedy Gloves

The King will reply, 'Truly I tell you, whatever you did for one of the least of these brothers and sisters of mine, you did for me."
Matthew 25:40 NIV

It's the most wonderful time of year. Yes, Christmas will soon upon us and my family and I are heading out to participate in one of our favorite family traditions. Each year, we give homemade Christmas cards to the elderly in a nearby nursing home and then take fruit to the local soup kitchen.

This winter has been particularly frigid so we decide to gather some coats, blankets, and gloves to deliver as well. I am rummaging through closets to find any items that may be useful to the homeless. In a basket I find a variety of new fluffy gloves in vibrant colors. I remember buying the stash of gloves on sale for around two dollars a pair. I pride myself in being a bargain hunter. "These are brand new gloves. I love this color and they will go nicely with my teal scarf. I just can't give these up." Those thoughts flooded my mind continuously. Greedy thoughts... sinful thoughts... I manage to talk myself into parting with several less desirable pairs and put the others back in the basket.

Later at the soup kitchen, my heart broke as I saw the thankfulness of those receiving our humble, small gifts of warmth for winter. These people had nothing and at the time, I seemed to have everything. I had been blessed with so much and yet couldn't bring myself to let go of a pair of new, two dollar gloves. Greedy gloves is how I refer to them but really my heart was the culprit, the covetous one.

I am reminded of a verse of Scripture from Matthew saying, "The King will reply, 'Truly I tell you, whatever you did for one of the least of these brothers and sisters of mine, you did for me.'" Those words pierce my heart as I realize God is saying to me,

"Can you not do this for me, after all that I have done for you? Think of all that I have given up for you, my only son…"

I am ashamed and disheartened at my selfishness and thankful God used the situation to teach me a lesson. Maybe you, too, have some "greedy gloves" in your closet. Perhaps there is a selfish attitude that is invading your heart. Give it over to Jesus and ask for forgiveness. None of us have room for greedy gloves in our lives.

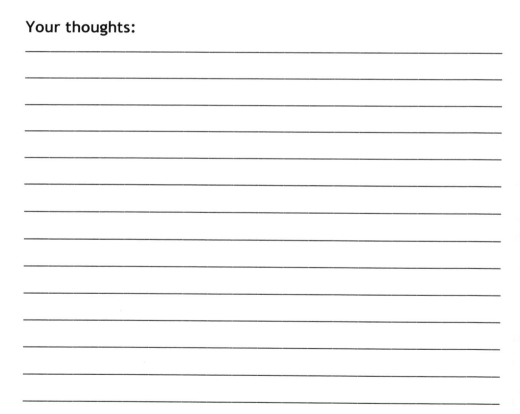

Your thoughts:

_____

_____

_____

_____

_____

_____

_____

_____

_____

_____

_____

_____

_____

_____

~Twenty~

An App for That

"Repent, then, turn to God, so that your sins may be wiped out, that times of refreshing may come from the Lord..."
Acts 3:19 NIV

"There's an app for that."

I have heard those words quite often and never have they been truer than now. Recently, my daughter showed me an app on her phone that allows you to tweak photos. For instance, if you feel that you look a little too chunky, chisel your cheeks for a slimmer appearance. Have under eye circles? Just wave the correcting wand in that area and "POOF!" No more circles. Freckles? Get rid of them with a touch of a button. Any imperfection that you dislike can be eliminated by the features on your phone or computer.

After playing around with this app with my daughter, I pondered, "Wouldn't it be nice if there was an app for your heart?" Any sin, anger, greed, or distrust in your heart? Use the app to get it taken care of. But wait...I do not need an app to handle all those impurities. As a born again believer in Jesus Christ, I am assured He has already paid the debt of my sins by His blood shed on the cross.

The Bible tells us in Acts that God completely wipes away our imperfections if we repent and turn to Him. Forgiveness that leads to refreshment of our hearts, deep cleansing, can be ours. We just need to ask for forgiveness—no app needed. Once we ask for forgiveness, then we must cling to God so He can continue to help us overcome our sin.

So for now, there's not a magic heart app. But I am so thankful God loves me enough to take care of my heart like no other can. I am learning in the process of confessing my sin and leaning on Him, my heart is growing like I never imagined possible. No application could ever do that.

Heavenly Father, please forgive the
sin in my heart. Make my heart clean
and pure in Your sight. Guide me in

a living a life that is pleasing and worthy of You. In Jesus' name I pray, Amen."

Your thoughts:

_____

_____

_____

_____

_____

_____

_____

_____

_____

_____

_____

_____

_____

_____

_____

~Twenty-One~

Heavenly Cheering Section

"In the day when I cried out, You answered me, and made me bold with strength in my soul." Psalm 138:3

My kids are blessed to have their own personal cheering sections at sporting events. My husband and I, as well as all their grandparents, make a special effort to make it to each event. Occasionally even an aunt or uncle will show up unexpectedly. During their games, we applaud and whoop and holler when my son makes a basket or my daughter returns the volleyball. We share in their excitement on the court and are there to provide encouragement, hopefully rallying them to victory.

As a believer in Christ, I have my own cheering squad for my game of life. God the Father, Jesus the Son, the Holy Spirit, and the multitude of believers in Heaven make up my personal group of supporters. They are constantly there for me in all my endeavors. In Psalm, I read, "In the day when I cried out, You answered me, and made me bold with strength in my soul." My group of encouragers celebrate when I'm experiencing the mountain tops of life but also to give help in the valleys.

When you feel stressed out from a busy day, your Heavenly cheering squad is there rooting you on, encouraging you to not give up. When you are scared to step out in faith and start that Bible study God's been calling you to lead, they are there to infuse you with courage. When you yelled at your kids for no reason at all, your cheering section is there to comfort you and give hope for second chances. Your Heavenly cheering squad shows up all the time to cultivate the strength you need to get through your game of life.

Thank God today for His blessing of your Heavenly cheering squad. Remember to talk to the Lord when you are facing struggles and when all is going well for you, as He wants to be involved in every aspect of your life. Tell someone today about the difference God has made in your life and the comfort your Heavenly cheering section provides.

Your thoughts:

_____

_____

_____

_____

_____

_____

_____

_____

_____

_____

_____

_____

_____

_____

_____

_____

_____

_____

_____

_____

~Twenty-Two~

Brown Bear Blunders

Come close to God, and God will come close to you...
James 4:8 NLT

Brown bears are so cute, aren't they? I recently watched a documentary on the life of a mother bear and her twin cubs in Alaska. The program focused on the critters' lives over the course of one year. It was truly fascinating to watch all the adventures the tiny family faced in the Artic. It was easy to surmise the mother bear had her paws full with the cubs, particularly the boy. The girl cub always wanted to be right with her mom, even riding on her back at times. She never strayed too far away from the comfort of her loving mom.

The boy cub had a much more adventurous spirit. Countless times, he found himself in frightening blunders because he chose to go his own way, straying from the safety of his mother. Often she had to rescue her son by fighting predators or searching for him when he got lost. There was no limit to what this mom would do for her offspring.

The documentary reminded me of my own life and relationship with my Heavenly Father. I have often been like the boy cub, wandering too far from the One who is my refuge. If I could just learn to stay close to my Father, I would be so much better off.

James 4:8 reminds me the way to have a deeper, closer relationship with the Lord is by moving closer to Him. But what exactly does it mean to move closer to God? I know from experience the only way for me to move toward God is by spending time with Him through prayer and reading the Bible, getting to know Him better. When I'm faithful with progressing toward Him, I can feel His presence and strength.

On the contrary, when I'm lax in devoting time to God, I can feel myself drifting down the wrong path, just as the little boy cub did so many times. The most comforting thought is that God loves us no matter if we stay close or stray. He will always be our protector and friend, nurturing us along the way.

Perhaps there have been times in your life when you have wandered just as the boy cub and I have done. Ask God for forgiveness and then commit to drawing closer to Him. Find hope in knowing God's grace abounds, even when we make mistakes.

Your thoughts:

_____

_____

_____

_____

_____

_____

_____

_____

_____

_____

_____

_____

_____

_____

_____

_____

_____

~Twenty-Three~

Love Them Like Family

Be devoted to one another in love. Honor one another above yourselves. Romans 12:10 NIV

"Don't get too attached," warned my friends and family about my physical therapy patients. In my heart, I know their cautioning words are given because they don't want to see me get hurt. However, I love my patients as if they are my family.

My geriatric clients usually welcome me into their world with open arms. I come into their home to help them physically get stronger and most times, they help me get stronger too, either emotionally or spiritually.

I know God has placed me in this career to minister to these homebound people. I cannot help but love them with all of my heart. When they go through trying times, so do I. When they are having a not-so-good day, so do I. Together we rejoice over news of the birth of a great-grandbaby and the rest of life's journeys—the ups and the downs.

Recently, a former patient passed away. I felt heart broken, as if a piece of me died too. I worked with this dear woman for many months and developed a special bond with her. I kept in touch even after she was discharged. It saddened me to think of a world without her gentle Christian spirit in it.

I was reminded of my loved ones' advice "Don't get too attached." Were they right? Was I setting myself up for heartbreak by caring too much?

The Lord brought a Scripture passage to mind that gave me the answer I needed. In Romans, I read, "Be devoted to one another in love. Honor one another above yourselves."

God calls us to be committed to loving others. He doesn't just want us to be loyal to our closest friends and family. He challenges us to love everyone, from the sweet neighbor down the street to your not-so-friendly co-worker. After all, as believers in Jesus Christ, aren't we all brothers and sisters anyway? We are all family, related by the blood shed for us on the cross so long ago.

What's more, God desires for us to love with a deep, devoted love. The kind that prompts you to take time out of your hectic day to counsel a friend who's trying to make a life-changing decision. Or the love that inspires you to dedicate your Saturday working in a soup kitchen serving the less fortunate.

It means we give of ourselves and try to help others become better people. Genuine, sincere love is what we are to give others. And sometimes that love requires you to sacrifice something precious, like your heart, as you grieve the loss of a cherished patient and friend.

In the end, loving others as God calls us to is worth it. Even though you may have to make sacrifices and risk the chance of getting hurt, the blessings of the relationship far outweigh the sacrifice. God will provide you with abundant peace, knowing you followed His command.

So go ahead—it's okay to get attached to those around you. Get involved with other people in your community, your workplace, your home. Seek out those who need to be loved and resolve to express love in meaningful ways. Ask God to help you learn to love everyone like family.

Your thoughts:

_____

_____

_____

_____

_____

_____

_____

_____

~Twenty-Four~

Rise and Shine

In the same way, let your light shine before others, so that they may see your good works and give glory to your Father who is in Heaven. Matthew 5:16 ESV

"Rise and shine. It's time to face the day so rise and shine." My mom woke me up every morning with these words when I was a young child. It was our little ritual of sorts, to let me know it was time to get the day started. Her words helped me begin my day with positivity.

I never thought of the words as having deeper meaning until recently. I came across the Scripture from Matthew as Jesus is teaching His disciples about being a light for Him. He encourages His followers to let the lights of their souls shine. He desires our lights glow so radiantly and brightly it attracts others so we can show them what Christ is like.

When the Holy Spirit lives within us, our light should not be hidden. The whole point for having and sharing our light is so that we can point to God, not ourselves.

But how can we ensure we are letting our lights shine to their fullest potential? To help our luminosity burn bright and strong for Him, we can stand up for what we know is true from a Biblical perspective. We can be bold, not giving in to peer pressure or going along with the crowd. We can be accepting of the light that Jesus offers us through His sacrifice on the cross. We should guard our hearts from sin creeping in, threatening to dim our blaze. Being a witness, sharing our testimony, helping those in need and giving of ourselves will illuminate God's light.

What can you do to let your light shine for God? Are there opportunities you may be missing out on that you could be helping lead others to God's light?

Pray God will help you "Rise and Shine" each day for Him, giving Him the glory and praise He deserves.

Your thoughts:

_____

_____

_____

_____

_____

_____

_____

_____

_____

_____

_____

_____

_____

_____

_____

_____

_____

_____

_____

_____

_____

_____

~Twenty-Five~

Cotton Fields

So we fix our eyes not on what is seen, but on what is unseen. For what is seen is temporary, but what is unseen is eternal.
2 Corinthians 4:18 NIV

Sometimes it seems that I live in my car. The miles seem countless as I journey to patients' homes to provide physical therapy. Most days I ride down some beautiful country roads, and particularly in autumn, the outdoor scenery is gorgeous. Imagine my surprise as a white, snow covered field catches my eye in the distance on my afternoon drive, one I've completed dozens of times.

The field is covered in a pearly snow blanket which contrasts vividly against the backdrop of colorful hues of burgundy, orange, and yellow leaves. Of course, as I get closer, I distinguish that what I'm seeing isn't snow, but cotton. A beautiful, fluffy cotton field is easily seen now. I can easily view the different parts of the cotton crop as I drive by. It's amazing how the field deceived me from a distance.

Viewing this cotton field prompted me to think about how the "cotton fields" of my life can be misleading. There are times when things or situations looked totally different from a distance. For example, I have judged people from their outward appearance thus giving me a certain opinion. But when I got to know the person by spending time with them, sometimes my perspective was altered. I have been proven wrong about a person's character or personality, simply because they looked different from a distance.

The same is true about my faith. There are times when I struggle with attempting what God is prompting me to do simply because it looks intimidating from a distance. However, if I have the courage to follow God's plan, what I'm aspiring to do, looks so much different up close. Through God's help and guidance, these "cotton fields" of life are easier to handle.

     The Bible encourages us to fix our eyes on God and He will give us a new perspective. Pray that God will make His will for your life evident to you. What is God calling you to do for Him? Obey His calling and be prepared to be bountifully blessed. Let Him use those "cotton fields" in your life to give you fresh perspective that will mold you into the person He intended you to be.

Your thoughts:

_____

_____

_____

_____

_____

_____

_____

_____

_____

_____

_____

_____

_____

_____

_____

~Twenty-Six~

Eating Machine

Take to heart all the words I have solemnly declared to you this day, so that you may command your children to obey carefully all the words of this law. They are not just idle words for you- they are your life.   Deuteronomy 32: 46-47 NIV

My 13-year-old son is an eating machine. He is 6' and wears a size fourteen shoe. He has been growing like a weed and doesn't seem to be stopping anytime soon. I am constantly asked the question of where my child gets his height? I always reply "I honestly don't know but I'm not complaining—he loves to play basketball".

Especially during growth spurts, Zack can put away some food. He doesn't discriminate either. My son will eat meats, sweets, fruits, vegies, breads, you name it, he wants it. There are days that it seems I don't even step foot out of my kitchen because of his constant state of hunger. Even after eating a huge meal, my son scrounges in the pantry to find more food. He has an appetite that cannot be satisfied. In his words, he is "starving". He always needs just a little bit more...

Wouldn't it be great if I was starving too? No, not starving from being on the latest fad diet. But starving to dig deeper into God's Word. How wonderful it would be if I had an enormous appetite for studying the Bible and praying. I petition the Lord to bless me with a hunger to know Him in a deeper, more personal way. To never be satisfied—always wanting more.

I love the passage of scripture from Deuteronomy describing when Moses talked to the Israelites about God's Word. He told the people the Scriptures were meant to be studied so they can be applied in their lives and passed on to others. That's a good reminder for me also. The Bible isn't filled with idle words. Those words require action. I need to learn more of God's Word so I can diligently share it with others.

I hope my children will discover the importance of reading and applying the scriptures to everyday life. Hopefully a steady diet of the Bible will keep them spiritually healthy. Pray today that God will lavish a spiritual hunger on you that will foster your growth and maturity in His grace. Petition the Lord to mold you into an "eating machine" of His Word.

Your thoughts:

_____

_____

_____

_____

_____

_____

_____

_____

_____

_____

_____

_____

_____

_____

_____

_____

_____

_____

~Twenty-Seven~

Middle School Faith

Pray also for me, that whenever I speak, words may be given to me so that I will fearlessly make known the mystery of the gospel. Ephesians 6:19 NIV

Every new school year brings a different set of challenges and experiences. This was especially true for my daughter, Abby, in her first year of middle school. New teachers, wider variety of friends, and changing classes made for a lot of adjusting on her part. However, she met the challenges with abundant grace and beauty.

One of her first assignments in her Communications class was to design a logo that represented her. The logo would be displayed to the class and accompanied by an oral presentation.

In a time when Abby was uncertain about friendships and middle school social status, she chose to be bold for Jesus. Her logo was a beautiful cross sitting upon a hill with the golden sun radiating beams of light onto the ground—simple but profound.

She stood in front of her peers and said, "I chose this logo that I made because I love God! He died on the cross for our sins and forgave all of us for all the wrong and bad things we have done. He is more than great, He is amazing. I hope you liked my logo. I hope you are also a believer in Christ. He saved and He will save again."

What a testimony she gave to God that day! At a time when she could have chosen to feel shy, she chose to stand up for Jesus in front of her classmates. Not only did she profess to be a Christian, but in her simple words she witnessed to her friends.

Her presentation reminds me of a verse from Ephesians: "Pray also for me, that whenever I speak, words may be given me so that I will fearlessly make known the mystery of the gospel."

This key verse emphasizes the importance of leading others to Jesus without fear or dread. Paul wrote this to the Ephesians while in prison and facing major struggles. However, he didn't ask that he be freed, but requested to continue to speak fearlessly for Christ, despite his current circumstances. Paul didn't fear persecution for his beliefs. He focused on bringing others to Christ. Only having confidence in Jesus could lead him to behave this way.

It's uncertain if Abby's cross logo presentation led any of her classmates to God. But I do know her logo changed my heart. Her faith and determination, sparked by God, has led me to examine myself closely and be encouraged to stand up for Jesus courageously. I can only hope to be the witness in my own life she has already been in her short twelve years.

Pray today that God will help you be bold in your witness as Paul and Abby have been. Be encouraged to stand up for what is Biblically true and right in God's eyes. Make a commitment to share your story with others. You may not have a specially designed logo like Abby, but you have words many others so desperately need to hear.

Your thoughts:

_____

_____

_____

_____

_____

_____

_____

_____

~Twenty-Eight~

Palm Tree Troubles

He gives strength to the weary and increases the power of the weak. Isaiah 40:29

We recently vacationed in Florida and stayed at a lovely resort. When we drove up the circle driveway, the first thing I spotted were the magnificent palm trees that lined the sidewalk Each tree's trunk was braced by several boards that provided extra support.

Apparently, palm trees can be fragile and prone to topple, especially if newly planted. It could be because their root structure hasn't had time develop or perhaps because of high winds Whatever the reason, the trees need extra support to help them stand tall.

Sometimes the winds of life attempt to knock me down and I, like the palm tree, need extra support. However, a Scripture in Isaiah reminds me, "He gives strength to the weary and increases the power of the weak."

God is there to help hold me up with His strength and power that never diminish. Even when the circumstances and failures of every day threaten to weaken my soul, the Lord gives me fortitude. He will always be there to brace me with His love and presence.

Rely on God in the storms of life. Grasp more of His stability today by digging deeper into His Word and spending time with Him in prayer.

❦

Your thoughts:

_____

_____

_____

_____

~Twenty-Nine~

The "Good" Scissors

As iron sharpens iron, so one person sharpens another.
Proverbs 27:17 NIV

I grew up with a crafty mom. She was always creating something. Whether it be cross stich, sewing, or ceramics, you could always count on her to make something special. Living with a crafty mom comes with a certain set of rules— the most important rule being "Do not use the 'good' scissors for anything other than fabric." The "good" scissors were specially sharpened and much more expensive than plain scissors. You didn't use the special scissors to cut paper or plastic because that would dull the blade and make them useless. So when I had a school project or wanted to cut pictures of my teen crush out of magazines, I had to use the regular scissors. That was my mom's rule and I tried my best to abide by it.

Thinking back, Mom packed a lot of wisdom in that one rule. Perhaps she was preparing me for my walk with God.

The Lord wants me to continually stay spiritually sharp. He desires my spiritual blade to be keen so my faith does not become dull. Just like Mom's good scissors, my spiritual walk can become useless to God if I'm not persistent in keeping it as razor-sharp as possible.

The Bible says in Proverbs, "As iron sharpens iron, so one person sharpens another." One way for me to stay spiritually sharp is to surround myself with believers who will encourage me on my faith journey. I am blessed with a community of wonderful people who inspire me daily to grow spiritually. Those same people are also there to share in the hard times of life and supply advice. Positive influences in my life not only have a great impact on me but also on the kingdom of God.

I am learning to be intentional with setting aside time to be alone with God. Through devotions, Bible reading and prayer, I concentrate more on growing my relationship with the Lord. Journaling thoughts, prayer requests, and praises prove to motivate me to focus on how God is working in my life daily.

Enjoying time in God's beautiful creation of nature gives me a chance to reflect on how truly awesome He is. These peaceful times outdoors force me to slow down and revel in beauty that only He can create. All these things help me to feel closer to God, which in turn, file my blade into something that can be used by Him, for Him.

Make it a point today to seek God intentionally. Pray that your spiritual blade can be sharpened and renewed for the purpose God has set out before you. Be thankful for friends and family He has placed in your life to build you up and provide inspiration for your daily walk.

Find joy in knowing that even if your blade gets a little blunt from time to time, God can help you become the "good scissors" again.

Your thoughts:

_____

_____

_____

_____

_____

_____

_____

_____

~Thirty~

Satan and Lace

Be alert and of sober mind. Your enemy the devil prowls around like a roaring lion looking for someone to devour.
1 Peter 5:8 NIV

"Satan and Lace? What kind of a store is that, Mom? It sounds really weird," my young son, Zack, blurted. I peered at my children in the back seat of our SUV and noticed they both wore puzzled expressions. Zack had mistakenly misread the shop sign as we drove by on our way to the park.

Immediately, I became amused and started belly-laughing. I explained that the sign should read Satin and Lace, which is a formal and bridal wear store. We all chuckled about the blunder and talked about it for a good while to come.

My son's mistake prompted me to think about "Satan and Lace". My heart was touched as I thought about the meaning of these words. Even though you wouldn't normally think of Satan and lace as two paired things, I quickly realized they have more in common than I originally thought. After all, isn't that how Satan disguises himself in our lives? He takes our ugly sin and tries to cover it with something pretty, like lace. He tries to mask it by making it appear better than it truly is. We are deceived and distracted and before long, head over heels deep in sin.

According to 1 Peter, the devil is constantly searching for someone to devour. We are to always be alert to protect ourselves from this attack. Don't let yourself be fooled—Satan takes a little bit of sin, covers it with beauty, good feelings, or makes it seem harmless. He works hard to make it look as good as possible. But there is hope. You do not have to fight this battle alone. The Lord will be with you to give you strength and protection. By surrendering your life to God, you have already won the battle.

My son's confusion helped teach me a very valuable lesson.

Always pay close attention and be on guard. This is helpful in the prevention of reading errors but also for the prevention of Satan creeping into our lives, even if he's disguised in lace!

> *Lord, help give me strength to guard*
> *against Satan's schemes.*
> *Provide me with physical, emotional,*
> *mental, and spiritual protection in my*
> *life as I live for You.*
> *In Jesus' name I pray, Amen.*

Your thoughts:

_____

_____

_____

_____

_____

_____

_____

_____

_____

_____

_____

_____

_____

_____

_____

~Thirty-One~

The Skittle

A new commandment I give to you, that you love one another: just as I have loved you, you also are to love one another. By this all people will know that you are my disciples, if you have love for one another. John 13:34-35

We had a wonderful time on my son's field trip to the North Carolina State Fair. We looked at exhibits, played games and rode twirling rides. Exhausted and hungry, our group went in search of something to eat.

As we walked through the dense crowd, I heard someone yell, "Hey, lady, you in the bright pink shirt. You stand out more than a Skittle in an M&M box of candy!"

The game attendant was trying to reel me in to play the ring toss game at his booth. He certainly got my attention and my first thought, *What's wrong with my shirt? Is it really that bright?* Immediately I became self—conscious. I wondered if I looked ridiculous. Later, I just shrugged the attendant's comment off. I knew he was only trying to drum up business for his booth.

I loved my super-comfy shirt, but this guy's statement triggered something else in me; I started thinking about the attendant's comment of me sticking out in the crowd. Initially, my attitude was negative but soon viewed things from a different perspective. Isn't it a compliment when I don't blend in with others? Don't I want to be different? Special? Unique?

I soon began to realize that's exactly what God desires. He wants us to stand out, not because of our clothes we wear, but by the lives we live for Him. He wants us to be different, distinguished by our Christian love toward others.

The Bible tells us in John, "A new commandment I give to you, that you love one another: just as I have loved you, you also are to love one another. By this all people will know that you are my disciples, if you have love for one another."

God is saying we are set apart by our actions of love toward others. We show that we belong to Him by the love we offer in our relationships and interactions with people, even strangers. Love is more than just warm fuzzy feelings. It reveals our identity to others.

When people look at you, do you stand out because of the love that you share? Do you set yourself apart from non-believers by practicing love every day? I hope I can answer yes to those questions but know there is still much room for improvement in those areas for me. For now, I don't mind if I stick out if that means that I'm working on setting myself apart for the right reasons. I will gladly be the Skittle in a world full of M&Ms.

Your thoughts:

_____

_____

_____

_____

_____

_____

_____

_____

_____

_____

_____

_____

_____

~Thirty-Two~

Princess Power

So in Christ Jesus you are all children of God through faith...
Galatians 3:26 NIV

Everywhere I looked, I saw princesses. My family and I were at Disney on vacation and we saw a multitude of beautiful princesses in every direction. Some were dressed as Cinderella in beautiful blue flowing gowns. Others had their hair fixed in cute little buns adorned with tiaras. Still yet, others had all the appropriate princess attire plus the attitudes that go along with it.

These precious girls reminded me of my daughter when she was around three or four. She loved to dress up like a princess at home. She had ball gowns and plastic high heeled shoes. She even had fluffy boas and wands to complete her look. I have many photos capturing those cherished moments in her life as she was absolutely adorable.

Now that she is twelve, going on twenty, I aspire she realizes her identity as a real, bonafide princess. She is the daughter of God himself, adopted into His family as a Christian believer. She truly is royalty and has a rich inheritance waiting for her. Galatians 3:26 reminds me, "So in Christ Jesus you are all children of God through faith," I am excited for my daughter as she has already made a profession of faith and is growing in her relationship with Jesus every day.

However, the trying teenage years are just around the corner. A time when she may have insecurities and questions about where she fits in with her peers. I pray she will hold onto the promise she is loved as a daughter by the One True King. Hopefully this will help her navigate through those turbulent years with confidence. She was a princess at three years of age and will continue to be one throughout eternity.

Find hope today that no matter how the world sees you, the Lord of the Universe views you as His precious child. He sacrificed so much that you might spend eternity with Him, living as royalty.

Your thoughts:

_____

_____

_____

_____

_____

_____

_____

_____

_____

_____

_____

_____

_____

_____

_____

_____

_____

_____

_____

_____

~Thirty-Three~

Road Signs

You make known to me the path of life...   Psalm 16:11 NIV

My fourteen-year-old son is getting ready to take driver's education at school. Heaven help me! When we drive together, I make extra efforts to point out road signs and discuss their meanings. I hope this will give my son an extra edge when he begins the driving class. As a "seasoned" driver, I tend to forget how important the signs are and take them for granted because I am used to seeing them all the time. Helping Zack recognize them has given me new perspective on how vital they are for driving safety.

I am prompted to think, *Wouldn't it be nice if my life had road signs to help me navigate safely*? There would be warning signs of a curve ahead, signifying trials that may lead me off the straight path. Maybe octagonal red stop signs that encouraged me to slow down or stop so I don't live my life in such a rush, missing the true beauty of God all around me. White no U-turn signs would remind me not to live in the past and focus on the hope of my future in Jesus Christ. No matter the sign, each one was designed for my safety and steering me in the appropriate direction of my desired destination.

The Bible reminds me in Psalm, "You make known to me the path of life." This verse reinforces God and His word act as road signs all around me, guiding me in the right direction.

Sometimes His signs are hard to see but I am confident He is always there to direct me. Many times, I think I can navigate life on my own and have everything under control. I sometimes neglect seeking God's advice and will for my life. That's when the road becomes treacherous and I get lost because of my own stubbornness. Losing my way is painful but God never promises we will have an easy road to travel, only that He will be there to guide us continually. My focus must be on Him so I can read the road signs He has laid out before me.

You may also be traveling down a difficult road right now. Perhaps you long for the crystal-clear road signs providing direction. Be encouraged that God will steer you right. Seek Him in all situations and He will not let you down. Pray diligently for discernment of the road signs God puts along your path for route to your destination, abundant peace and intimately knowing Him.

Your thoughts:

_____

_____

_____

_____

_____

_____

_____

_____

_____

_____

_____

_____

_____

_____

_____

~Thirty-Four~

I Live You

May God himself, the God of peace, sanctify you through and through. May your whole spirit, soul, and body be kept blameless at the coming of our Lord Jesus Christ.
1 Thessalonians 5:23 NIV

I admit it. I have never enjoyed talking on the phone, but I enjoy texting—it's my favorite form of communication. It's nice to be able to text my husband a cute message letting him know that I'm thinking of him or sending messages to my children just to say "I love you" or that I'm proud of them.

Often when I send my text messages, I will use the phrase "I love you". However, most times I inevitably mistype love and it comes out as "live". So my phrase will read, "I live you". Then I must go back and correct my mistake so that it makes sense. I'm always mistyping it because the *I* and the *O* are right beside each other on the keypad and I hit the wrong button. Sometimes I get so frustrated with myself because I make the same mistake repeatedly.

Recently though, I was thinking there is possibly more to the phrase "I live you" than just a typing error. I was convinced this was happening for a reason. Perhaps it was a reminder from God that I needed to "live" Him. Not only do I need to love Him with all my heart but I should aspire to live for Him in my everyday life. I need to live in a way that points others to Him.

If I could send a text message to God, I can think of no better message to send than the words "I live you". I want my actions and words to reflect Him in my life. I pray that my attitude and the way I treat others will show that Jesus lives within me. I hope that even the inner reflections of my heart will be evidence of living Jesus in my day to day life.

I make plenty of mistakes—not just typing mistakes. I fail at treating others kindly or have a bad attitude in certain situations. But I'm praying that in those times, God will touch my heart again and remind me that I may be the only Jesus that some people will see. If I don't live Jesus, I may miss an opportunity to lead someone to Christ or even worse, lead them away from Christ.

I want others to see I genuinely live for God, bringing Him glory. I am confident God places high value on the phrase "I live you" as evidence is stated in the Scriptures. Paul tells us in 1 Thessalonians, "May God Himself, the God of peace, sanctify you through and through. May your whole spirit, soul, and body be kept blameless at the coming of our Lord Jesus Christ." This was Paul's way of reminding us that God must be involved in every aspect of our life, every part of how we live. By "living Jesus", we can express our love to our wonderful Father and show He is the authority over us.

Resolve today to let God be in control of every part of your life. Seek out opportunities to "live Jesus" and be a witness for Him. Know that when you make a mistake, God is there to lovingly help you get back on track so you can once again say "I live you."

Your thoughts:

_____

_____

_____

_____

_____

_____

~Thirty-Five~

Knock, Knock

Ask and it will be given to you; seek and you will find; knock and the door will be opened to you.
Matthew 7:7 NIV

I am 38 years-old and a major chicken when it comes to opening the door to strangers. It sounds silly, but it's true. When I'm home alone and the doorbell rings, I cringe. *Who could that be? Is it someone I know? What do they want?* are some of the questions that flood my mind. Fear of the unknown unsettles my soul and makes my palms sweat. I peer out the kitchen window, trying to get a glimpse of the visitor. Sometimes I crawl on my hands and knees to get a better view of the front porch without being detected. Ridiculous, I know. But I just can't help it. I always have and always will be a major chicken when it comes to opening doors.

I'm reminded of a scripture in Matthew that refers to believers knocking on the door. "Ask and it will be given to you; seek and you will find; knock and the door will be opened to you." In this passage we are promised that if we knock, the door will be opened for us. God is not standing on the other side, petrified to let us in—like me. Excitedly, He welcomes us with open arms and invites us to commune with Him. God desires to share His intimate thoughts and feelings with us. He is waiting on the other side of the door, ready to reveal more of Himself as we spend time in His presence.

Be persistent in knocking on the door of God. He wants us to actively seek Him and in the process, bless us with increased faith, focus and determination. He will always be there to open the door for you, welcoming you into His presence with a warm embrace.

Your thoughts:

_____

_____

_____

_____

_____

_____

_____

_____

_____

_____

_____

_____

_____

_____

_____

_____

_____

_____

_____

_____

_____

_____

_____

_____

_____

~Thirty-Six~

Stench-Filled House

The Lord himself goes before you and will be with you; he will never leave you nor forsake you. Do not be afraid; do not be discouraged. Deuteronomy 31:8 NIV

"Trust me, you will want to wear a gown and gloves when you go in the house," a co-worker advised. That forewarned me I was about to go into a horrible living situation. I love my job as a Home Health Physical Therapy Assistant. I feel blessed to help those in need, but I dislike home situations where there is filth or structural safety issues. I was nervous as I drove to my new patient's house.

What would I encounter while there? How bad was the house going to be? I wondered. *Would I even be able to help my patient in these living conditions?*

Minutes later, as I arrived at the humble home, God whispered words from Deuteronomy. "The Lord Himself goes before you and will be with you; he will not leave you nor forsake you. Do not be afraid; do not be discouraged."

Thank you, Lord, for this reminder. God has already been where I am going to prepare the way for me. He will be with me no matter where I go. The Lord will be with me in this house, helping me, encouraging me to be brave. I was inspired by God's words and completed my physical therapy visit in less than desirable conditions. As it turns out, my patient that day was one of the sweetest ladies I've ever met. I was happy to have been able to help her. Later, in bed, as I thought over the day, I was overwhelmed to think of the Holy Spirit being in that place with me—that dirty, dark house where He doesn't belong. God showed me again that He doesn't just go with us to life's happy houses— ones with white picket fences and sparkling clean floors. He is also there in the stench-filled houses with clutter and soiled furniture.

Be uplifted that God will be with you no matter what your day holds or wherever you may go. He promises to never leave your side.

Your thoughts:

_____

_____

_____

_____

_____

_____

_____

_____

_____

_____

_____

_____

_____

_____

_____

_____

_____

_____

~Thirty-Seven~

Family Photo

But to all who believed him and accepted him,
he gave the right to become children of God.
John 1:12 NLT

I do not like to attend funeral services. I am not sure if anyone does. However, I received a special blessing at the visitation service for a friend's dear mother. While waiting in line, I was privileged to view some photos of the deceased lady and her family. Photography is a passion of mine—naturally these pictures caught my eye immediately.

The family represented their loved one with a display table of portraits and treasured items. There were dignified self-portraits and candid group shots. Numerous wedding photos and snapshots of grandchildren adorned the special table. I enjoyed looking at every one of those precious memories. My heart warmed at the loving tribute that was given to this woman's life. The photo that most caught my attention was that of her whole family. All four of her children and countless grandchildren were posing for this one family photo. I was intrigued thinking of all the different personalities and age groups represented in this picture. It was evident to see the love these people shared—they were family.

I thought about this picture for a long time and wondered why I loved it so much. It reminded me of my faith. One day, I will be posing for the most wonderful family photo ever, the one in Heaven with my Christian brothers and sisters.

John 1:12 reminds us that as believers, we are children of God, His family. How exciting it is to ponder being together and posing with our Heavenly Father for that group shot. It's even more compelling to know that God will treasure this photo because of the love that is shared between us. I imagine He will value it so much that it will be framed in an ornate, gold frame.

Can't you just visualize God searching for the perfect spot on His wall to hang the portrait?

Join me in knowing we are part of God's most precious group. Do you have a reservation to have your picture taken with the King? I am hoping you will be right beside me, grinning from ear-to-ear in that Heavenly family photo.

Your thoughts:

_____

_____

_____

_____

_____

_____

_____

_____

_____

_____

_____

_____

_____

_____

_____

_____

_____

_____

~Thirty-Eight~

Lazy Gardener

The soul of the sluggard craves and gets nothing, while the soul of the diligent is richly supplied. Proverbs 13:4 ESV

I dream of having a gorgeous flower garden. There are lush hydrangea bushes bringing forth blossoms of blue and lavender. Brilliant buttercups line the edging of the garden while pansies daintily sprout close to the ground. My garden is breathtaking and invites you to abide there all day.

My real garden pales in comparison. No buttercups or hydrangeas bloom because I haven't taken the time to plant them. The flowers and bushes growing are sparse, lacking the attention of one with a green thumb. I admit I am a lazy gardener. I want the benefits and beauty of a wondrous flower garden but don't want to invest the time or energy to foster one.

I wonder, *Am I a lazy gardener when it comes to my personal walk with God? Do I want all the benefits of a close relationship with Him without devoting myself to Him*? I want to cultivate the "flowers" (love, joy, peace etc.) of my faith.

Proverbs teaches that if I want to prosper in my relationship with my Savior, I cannot be sluggish. I must be diligent in spending time with Him so I can know Him better.

Perhaps you feel a little sluggish too in your walk with God. Resolve today to devote more time getting to know the One who created you and all the flowers on earth. Commit to reading your Bible and spending quality time in prayer. Let God help you develop your faith into the garden of your dreams.

Heavenly Father, forgive me
as I have made mistakes in
my walk with You. Please help
me to mature and grow in my
faith in You. In Jesus' name, Amen.

Your thoughts:

_____

_____

_____

_____

_____

_____

_____

_____

_____

_____

_____

_____

_____

_____

_____

_____

_____

_____

_____

_____

_____

_____

_____

_____

~Thirty-Nine~

Sunday Morning Scramble

For I the Lord do not change; therefore you, O children of Jacob, are not consumed. Malachi 3:6 NIV

It was Sunday Morning straight out of an Erma Brombeck book, beginning with my hitting the snooze button one too many times. My children seemed to be having a contest with snails to see who could move slower. The cat insisted on running inside and playing hide-n-seek behind the furniture. Never one to outdone by the family feline, our dog decorated my pants with muddy pawprints-my pants for church.

I hurried into the bathroom to scrub the mud away quickly. "We're already late for church and I needed to be there early to make copies for my Sunday School class," I snapped at my husband who was still getting ready.

My attitude was bad and I couldn't help but be in a sour mood as we drove to church. I felt rushed and honestly worshiping God was the last thing on my mind.

During those times things can get hectic. But there is hope for the chaotic Sunday morning scramble.

In Malachi, I read, "For I the Lord do not change; therefore you, O children of Jacob, are not consumed." This key verse reminds me that God always has and always will be the same. He is the constant in my messy, rushed, topsy-turvy world. He is there for protection from the evil one who's only desire is to consume me.

I have no doubt Satan likes to put distractions in my way. If he can divert my attention to my problems and away from God, like being late for church, he renders me ineffective for the kingdom of God. If I have such a bad attitude that I cannot focus on worshipping and praising God, Satan has been successful. He only wants to consume the light I can be for God.

Don't let Satan put you in a crazy whirlwind, losing sight of what is important. Do all you can to prepare yourself but realize God is in control. Things will happen that will turn your world upside down, but know God is your peace in the storms of life. Pray for patience and will to remain an effective witness even in the Sunday morning scramble.

> *Lord, please give me patience and the*
> *will to remain an effective witness for*
> *You. Help provide tranquility in my life,*
> *even on those days when I feel rushed*
> *and chaos threatens to surround me.*
> *Let me feel Your calming presence always.*
> *In Jesus' name, Amen.*

Your thoughts:

_____

_____

_____

_____

_____

_____

_____

_____

_____

_____

~Forty~

Priceless Doll

For you are a people holy to the Lord your God. The Lord your God has chosen you out of all the peoples on the face of the earth to be his people, his treasured possession.
Deuteronomy 7:6 NIV

She was the most beautiful doll I had ever seen. A Christmas gift from my aunt, I loved this porcelain doll with all of my 7-year-old heart. She had lovely long, golden hair that cascaded down her shoulders and back. A fancy pink dress trimmed in blue and was just the right size for carrying-everywhere. I cherished the gift and all the memories made with her by my side for many years. To this day, I still have the doll tucked away safely at my house. And since my aunt recently passed away, she means more to me now more than ever.

I visited a local antique shop the other day and was surprised to see the very same doll for sale. She looked exactly like mine but wore a price tag of only two dollars. Two dollars? Is that all the shop owners thought she was worth? Surely the doll was worth much more than that? It saddened me to think the retailers failed to recognize the true value of this toy.

Sometimes we as believers fail to recognize our value in God's eyes. Poor self- esteem or failed relationships can cause us to doubt our worth and purpose. We may see ourselves as having very little value, nothing to offer. But God tells us something completely different in the book of Deuteronomy. In this passage, Moses addresses the Israelites as they prepare to destroy their enemies, "For you are a people holy to the Lord your God. The Lord your God has chosen you out of the peoples on the face of the earth to be his people, his treasured possession." Just as God chose the Israelites to be His sanctified people, we too can be part of His cherished possession. This verse confirms God's intense love for us, even so, to call us holy, or sacred, to Him. He values us so much not because of what we can do for Him but because of His wondrous goodness and grace that He chooses to lavish on us.

Stop viewing yourself in a negative light and see yourself as God intended—a beautiful masterpiece that is treasured by God. We all make mistakes and will feel bad about ourselves from time to time. But those negative thoughts demean our value and blur the perspective of how God truly sees us. None of us have time to waste seeing ourselves like the depreciated doll at the antique shop. Pray that God will help you see yourself as a treasured gift, just as I see the gift of my priceless childhood doll.

Your thoughts:

_____

_____

_____

_____

_____

_____

_____

_____

_____

_____

_____

_____

_____

~Forty-One~

True Trail Blazer of Life

...Make Your way straight before me. Psalm 5:8 (NIV)

On a mid-October afternoon, my husband and I walked through the woods of a national park, excited about our hiking adventure ahead of us. The cool air felt refreshing on our skin as we trudged through the trail entrance, laden with a backpack filled with water, bug repellent, and snacks. The sun shone brightly, mimicking our moods, as we viewed, from a distance, God's beautiful of colors in the sea of autumn trees. We continued walking slowly along the dirt boundary where trees were sparse and crossed a tiny bridge to the thicker forest.

As we hiked deeper into the woods, the compassing path became less visible due to leaves of red, gold, and orange that littered the ground. Our trail was disguised and very misleading as we now didn't know which direction to go. We had lost our way.

"Which way should we go?" I asked worriedly of my husband.

"Just keep going straight. We will eventually come back to where we started since this goes in a loop."

We kept marching on. My honey and I aimed straight and continued our feat in the woods. Even though we couldn't clearly see the path marked before us, we kept pressing on. Eventually, we found the trail's exit.

I am reminded of how situations in life resemble my hiking adventure that day. Sometimes for me, the right choice or direction in which my life should go are not so easily determined. The path is hidden by confusing leaves that distract, clutter, and throw me off course.

In those bewildering times, the best thing for me to do is pray as the Psalmist did. I cry out to God for His direction to be made known to me. I beseech the Lord to lay His will out before me so I may easily identify it.

God is always faithful to answer my prayers. He does not let me continue to wander aimlessly. I have discovered the Lord has something to teach me in those moments when I feel lost and confused. He uses the journey for preparation for the trail ahead. He has a plan for me even though my limited perception won't allow me to see it at the time.

God is true to His promises to never leave or forsake me and gives guidance for every day. He is gracious to lay the route out before me and offer help through all those tough adventures on the path of my existence. God is the true trail blazer of my life.

Heavenly Father, thank you for providing me with blessings in all shapes and sizes, even those situations that seem hard at the time. I am confident You use those times to shape and mold me into the person who is pleasing to You. Please guide me on the straight path that always leads directly to You. In Jesus' name I pray, Amen.

Your thoughts:

_____

_____

_____

_____

_____

_____

_____

~Forty-Two~

Sneaky Snoring Slumber Story

...Be still and know and know that I am God..."
Psalm 46:10 NIV

I lay awake, listening to the all too familiar sounds of snoring from my husband. Any other night, I would be tempted to go to the recliner in the den—anything to get away from the muffled snores that haunted me so many times. But not tonight...tonight was different. As I lay there, I started thinking about how my husband's snoring might actually be a blessing to me. After all, some of my best ideas and inspiration for writing have come to me while lying in bed, trying to go to sleep. Many nights I have talked to God, tossed and turned, huffed and puffed, but to no avail. No slumber for me!

Many times God uses those frustrating moments to inspire me to write another passage or reflect on things that have occurred during the day. He uses those things to encourage me and that gives me the desire to encourage others through my words. God might use that time to convict me of something I've done wrong so I can learn from the experience, helping me to grow spiritually. And sometimes I just lay there and think about all the things I need to put on my "To Do" list for the next day.

The point is, even though my husband's snoring is annoying, something good comes from my lack of sleep. I think about things I might not ordinarily think of during the day because I am so busy running from one task to another. In those times in bed, I am quiet and still and that's a blessing even if I'm not sleeping.

Isn't it just like God to work in our lives this way? In every situation, circumstance and decision we make, God is working those things for our good, our benefit.

We may be going through the worst possible thing imaginable and wondering *why*. Why do I have to go through this? Why do I have to face this obstacle? Why am I having so many problems? It's so easy to get caught up thinking negative thoughts and having a pity party. And believe me, I have been there before—MANY times.

Satan wants to be sneaky, tricking us into having these bad thoughts. But God is in control and everything you face is part of His plan. It may be hard to see at the time, but God can turn those horrible experiences in your life into something wonderful.   Just as I have always thought about my husband's snoring as a nuisance, God has shown me it might not be so bad after all. The same holds true for those problems you may be facing right now. God can use those difficult circumstances to work for good in your life and give you blessings. The key is to rely on Him and slow down enough to be still, so that you can recognize God working in your life.

According to Psalm 46:10, "...Be still and know that I am God..." God is telling us to be still, stop being so busy, and realize He is the Lord of our lives and is in complete control.

Be assured God is going to bless you through the tough times. Realize He is God when you can't fall asleep due to loud snoring. God provides hope we will get through those trying times and with luck, not be totally sleep deprived in the process.

Your thoughts:

_____

_____

_____

_____

_____

_____

_____

_____

_____

_____

~Forty-Three~

Releasing Her Hand to Safety

For I am the Lord your God who takes hold of your right hand and says to you, 'Do not fear; I will help you.
Isaiah 41:13 NIV

It was the chance of a lifetime for my eleven-year-old daughter, Abby. She won a scholarship to a basketball camp at North Carolina State University this past summer. As part of her camp experience, she had the opportunity to stay on campus in a dorm with a roommate for four days and three nights.

Did I mention that I didn't get to stay with her? Great opportunity for Abby but as her protective mom, a heart-wrenching time for me.

Abby, my husband, and I arrived at campus on the June check-in day with plenty of time to get my daughter settled in her modest dorm room. It supported two bunk beds, a small closet area, and a feeble desk. It seemed so cold and lonely. I couldn't imagine my sweet, full of life girl spending the next few days here by herself.

What if she needs me? What if she doesn't get along with her roommate? What if she gets sick? were just a few of the thoughts that scurried through my mind.

No, I wasn't ready to leave her just yet. We still had a lot more time together, or so I thought. We walked back to the gymnasium and spent our remaining time talking about all the exciting things she would be able to do in the upcoming week.

Suddenly, her leader appeared and whisked the girls into a straight line. Then they all started walking toward the door. My heart raced and I began to worry, *Were they leaving for good now? So soon? Don't I get a chance to say goodbye?*

I ran to catch up with Abby as she'd already made it outside now, walking down the sidewalk with her ponytail swishing happily.

I reached her in line and grabbed her precious hand. "I love you and I'm going to miss you so much," I whispered.

"I love you too, Mom," she replied. I pulled her hand in close to my chest, never letting go of my intense grip as we exchanged a quick hug.

I wanted to continue walking with her, holding her hand firmly. I didn't want to let go. I couldn't let go.
But I knew I had to.

The words from a Bible verse in Isaiah came to mind, "For I am the Lord your God who takes hold of your right hand and says to you, 'Do not fear; I will help you.'"

It was as if the Lord Himself was speaking to me saying, "Let her go. I will hold her hand and take care of her. Do not worry."

Even though it was one of the hardest things I've ever done in my life, I mustered up the courage to let go of my baby girl. As my eyes filled with tears, I released her hand and watched her continue to trot down the sidewalk on her new adventure.

My heart felt broken because I knew it would be an eternity before I would see my daughter again. How was she going to survive the week without me but also, how was I going to survive without her?

I clung to the Isaiah scripture the entire week Abby was at camp. It provided comfort and a safe haven for me during such an anxious period in my life. I was assured God was with Abby every step of the way. Every drill she practiced, meal she ate, conversation she spoke, He was there. God would never let go and she would be safe. He showed me I had to release Abby's hand to Him so that He could grasp it, easing her worries, leading her, protecting her.

And what's more, I grew in my relationship with God as I learned to trust in Him completely. By freeing my grasp on Abby, I was able to reach up toward the Lord, my fortress of safety and protection. Of course He was there to hold my right hand also, giving me strength and boldness to push through missing my girl so much.

Find peace in knowing that no matter what trials or circumstances you find yourself in today, God is there, holding onto you. Trust in Him to help you as He has promised to do.

Your thoughts:

_____

_____

_____

_____

_____

_____

_____

_____

_____

_____

_____

_____

_____

_____

_____

_____

_____

_____

_____

_____

~Forty-Four~

Spillage of Love

My command is this: Love each other as I have loved you."
John 15:12 NIV

"Don't spill the water, Abby," I say almost every morning. My daughter has a very important chore of feeding and providing water for our two cats before school. Inevitably, she ends up dribbling some of the water on the floor during her journey from the laundry room to the front porch. I admit that sometimes I am frustrated because of the spillage on the floor.

I recently heard a man giving his testimony on the radio. He talked about how we as Christians should have spillage of love onto other people. Hearing those words convicted my conscious. I have the completely wrong attitude about the water situation. Jesus tells us in the Bible "My command is this: Love each other as I have loved you." When on earth, Jesus provided the ultimate example of how to love one another. In every word spoken, every action taken, every thought penetrating his mind, he demonstrated complete love for us. Ultimately, Jesus submitted to the will of his Father as to pay the debt of our sins. He exhibited his spillage of love in the form of blood and water mingled together on the cross.

The greatest way for us to show Christ to others is to do as the verse says...love. Isn't that what my daughter was doing all along? Was she not showing love to me by completing her chore without complaining? Was she not showing love to her animals by providing for their needs? I can really learn a thing or two from my twelve-year-old child. I want my cup of love to be filled so full that it spills over onto everyone I see: my family; neighbors; church family; the people standing in line next to me at the store. Perhaps you, too, struggle with giving love freely to others. Pray that God will help you lavish your love onto others unselfishly. Make a commitment today to strive to share love in all situations, from the small things to the big things. Resolve that it's wonderful to have a messy spill, in this case, as it just may point others to Christ.

Your thoughts:

_____

_____

_____

_____

_____

_____

_____

_____

_____

_____

_____

_____

_____

_____

_____

_____

_____

_____

_____

_____

_____

_____

_____

~Forty-Five~

Tapestry of Life

For you created my inmost being, you knit me together in my mother's womb...My frame was not hidden from you when I was made in the secret place, when I was woven together in the depths of the earth. Psalm 139:13,15

My mom and mother-in-law have given me several quilts and tapestries as heirlooms to cherish. Each quilt was lovingly tale made by adding stitch-by-stitch and square-by-square together to produce a beautiful piece of art. When the thread and scraps of material are separate, they don't have much meaning. But when the weaver or quilter forms them together by sewing and stitching in a pattern, they become so much more—an elaborate tale created with fabric, stitches and love.

I can't help but think that each of my experiences are like squares or pieces of a quilt. Every friendship I've had, every disappointment incurred, every moment of happiness, every time I've felt God's presence, every choice I've made, all have been formed by God to create my life tapestry.

I often wonder what my life quilt will look like as I get older? What designs, patterns, colors and themes will my tapestry behold? How will my fabric look different from others? Will I be able to distinguish those times when I struggled from the moments of rejoicing by a change in the pattern or variation in color?

The Bible reinforces that God is the Master Weaver. I know God knitted me together in my mother's womb and wove me together in the depths of the earth. How precious I am to Him that created me, that He took such care to form me? Even more so now, I am cherished by Him as He continues to work in my life, piecing all my experiences together for His good, for His purposes. Whether there is sadness or happiness, when I choose to let God have His will in my life, He forms all of it into a wonderful tapestry for His glory. He turns my life into something useful for Him and His kingdom.

Eventually my days on earth will come to an end and my tapestry will be completed. I hope the fabric of my life will be even more beautiful than the quilts and weavings I have as heirlooms now. But most of all, I aspire when the Master Weaver reflects upon my tapestry, He will experience great joy and pride for the life I lived for Him.

Make a choice to abide in His will and watch as your beautiful story is woven into your incredible tapestry by the Master Weaver.

> *Lord, please design my life into*
> *The beautiful tapestry or quilt you*
> *desire it to be. Let me live inside*
> *Your will so that Your purposes will*
> *be accomplished. Give me peace*
> *when struggles and disappointments*
> *arise in life, that I may know you are*
> *weaving it all together to form my life's*
> *story that points to You. In Jesus' name,*
> *Amen.*

Your thoughts:

_____

_____

_____

_____

_____

_____

~Forty-Six~

Menacing Models

Do not let your adorning be external- the braiding of hair and the putting on of gold jewelry, or the clothing you wear- but let your adorning be the hidden person of the heart with imperishable beauty of a gentle and quiet spirit, which in God's sight is very precious. 1 Peter 3:3-4 ESV

I opened the mailbox and there it was...the dreaded bi-monthly clothing magazine. I'm not even sure how I came to acquire it, but like clockwork it arrives every two weeks to torture me. I flipped through the pages and saw an array of gorgeous models wearing stunning clothes. The women have perfect hair, makeup, bodies...perfect everything.

And then come the thoughts, *I wish I looked like her. Why can't my hair hold curl like that? She's skinny and fit. I will never look like that.* On and on the negative thoughts continue to penetrate my mind.

I play the comparison game between myself and these beautiful women constantly. And by comparing myself to those magazine models, I fall short every time and develop poor self-esteem.

It's not that I am unhappy with myself or the way I look, it's just that someone always looks so much better! What really scares me is the realization that if I struggle with this, chances are my twelve-year-old daughter probably will too.

To help me through these rough patches of self-worth, I focus on Scripture from 1 Peter reminding me God desires me to be more concerned with the beauty of my heart rather than my external beauty. Does that mean it's wrong for me to want to exercise to get healthier or lose weight? Absolutely not. Do the key verses imply it's wrong to want to look my best or love wearing makeup? Of course not.

The Bible verses inspire me not to get caught up in all those vain pursuits, to make them the focus of my attention. A beautiful heart is much more valuable and cherished by God than the prettiest of outward appearances. God knows that external beauty will fade, but a gorgeous heart will be everlasting.

Do not be discouraged when you see those perfect, menacing models in magazines. Let them serve as a reminder of the desire of our Heavenly Father to make our inner beauty far outshine our external beauty. Make a point to help your daughters and grand-daughters derive their self-esteem and worth from the Lord. And lastly, unsubscribe to those pesky magazines that keep coming in the mail every other week- after all, you, like me, have probably never ordered one of their outfits anyway!

Your thoughts:

_____

_____

_____

_____

_____

_____

_____

_____

_____

_____

_____

_____

_____

~Forty-Seven~

Crape Myrtle Tree of Love

It always protects, always trusts, always hopes, always perseveres. 1 Corinthians 13:7 NIV

My favorite wedding photo of my husband and I was taken outside our church in front of a gorgeous Crape Myrtle tree. The tree provided the perfect backdrop of green and dark pink. The ample blossoms hinted at the beautiful love that was shared between us and of the love to be shared in the years to come.

Almost twenty years later, we still go to the same church and walk by the tree frequently. I noticed the other day that the tree has been cut back for the winter. It was a sad sight to see as no pretty flowers, only shortened brown limbs sprouted up from the ground. If one didn't know better, you would think the tree was dead.

The Crape Myrtle holds sentimental value to me because of all it represented to a newly married young couple. The tree signified our love for each other, full and beautiful in every way. However, I can't help but think that the tree that symbolizes our marriage may not always look like the one pictured in the photo.

A few times, our tree of love might closely resemble the pruned tree that is in our church yard now. There have definitely been hard times in our marriage. We have not had a perfect union, as seldom anyone does. Plenty of mistakes have been made along our journey and at times, I have felt as though our love withered under the pressures of life. But even in those dormant seasons, we were persistent in loving God and loving each other.

Usually the trying times we experience yield a healthier marriage relationship, one that is encouraged to continue to grow and nurture each other. We cling to the verse about love in 1 Corinthians that says, "It always protects, always trusts, always hopes, always perseveres." This verse assures me the tree of love will blossom again, even if it seems hopeless. God can bring a renewing to marriage just as the hope of Spring and Summer bring new birth to His creation of plants and vegetation.

Pray that God will help you in your marriage, whether you are facing hard times or basking in the light of fresh love. God is there to help protect your union if you fully rely on Him. Do not give up and have persistent faith your marriage can be productive and healthy, just like the Crape Myrtle tree of love from my wedding day.

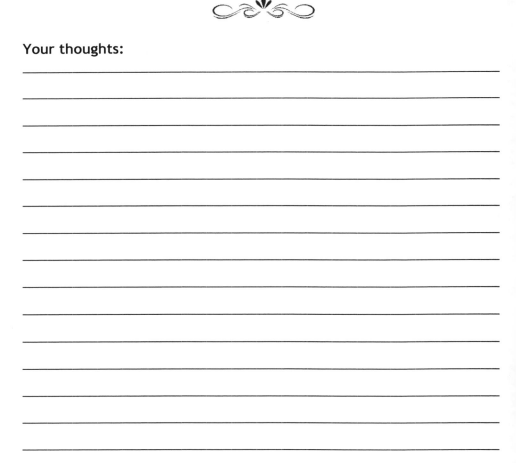

Your thoughts:

_____

_____

_____

_____

_____

_____

_____

_____

_____

_____

_____

_____

_____

_____

~Forty-Eight~

The Fight of Your Life

...And behold, I am with you always, to the very end of the age.
Matthew 28:20 ESV

"Who ever said these were the golden years, well, they lied," an elderly gentleman told me in the doctor's office. Even though I am not old enough to be considered geriatric, I have often found myself agreeing with this stranger's statement.

Specializing in home health physical therapy, I work with the geriatric population daily. I see first-hand the struggles they incur. Of course, They're receiving therapy because of some sort of physical weakness or problem, but most times, emotional, financial, relational, or neglect are among other problems that accompany their physical limitations.

Many times I find myself thinking, *Life just isn't fair. These elderly people should be relishing their last days not trudging through them as if anchored down by a one-hundred-pound weight.* Quite honestly, life puts up a fight to the very end. There will always be struggles and obstacles to overcome, even in our old age.

But there is always hope. It comes in the form of God, who is always with me. In Matthew, I am reminded God never leaves or forsakes me. There is no place I go or circumstance I'm in, that His love and presence cannot reach. Just knowing He is a friend and companion I can trust to be faithful is comforting to me.

I try to pass this encouragement onto my patients. For many, the long days would simply be unbearable without this hope. Peace is found in knowing God cares for them and is accompanying them on the journey of life forever- till the end of their days on earth and throughout eternity.

Lord, thank You for Your continual
presence in my life. Help me find

hope in Your promise You will always be with me, no matter where I go or what I do. Give me strength to fight the battle of life with grace and courage, knowing You are forevermore with me. Guide me in being an encourager to others, that they might know you more intimately. In Jesus' name I pray, Amen.

Your thoughts:

_____

_____

_____

_____

_____

_____

_____

_____

_____

_____

_____

_____

_____

_____

~Forty-nine~

Race Car Driver

Be on your guard; stand firm in the faith; be courageous; be strong. 1 Corinthians 16:13 NIV

My son thinks he is a race car driver. "When I turn sixteen, I'm going to speed up and down these roads."

I know my fourteen-and-half-year-old son was only joking to see how I would react. There we were...sitting in my car with my son in the driver's seat and me on the passenger side. Something is wrong with this picture. This should not be happening already. Just yesterday, wasn't I holding him in my arms and singing him to sleep?

Yet here we are—going on our first practice driving session in an abandoned church parking lot. We've gone over all the necessary items for safety and reviewed the mechanics of the car. We've even prayed together. We are ready to drive.

I am excited and nervous at the same time. My son put the car in drive and eased up on the brakes. Slowly he pushed the gas pedal and we glided across the parking lot. Suddenly, I realized that my life was truly in the hands of my child, totally dependent on him and his driving capabilities. I placed all my confidence in him to keep us safe. Zack will follow the rules of driving and prevail at this task. I have faith in him.

I am reminded of one of my favorite Bible verses from 1 Corinthians. "Be on your guard; stand firm in the faith; be courageous; be strong." I cling to this verse while I'm in the car with my son.

Lord please help me to have complete faith in You. I know that You will protect my son and give him discernment to make wise decisions. Grant me

*the wisdom to teach this child what
he needs to be safe. Help me to be
strong and courageous as I realize
that my only son is growing up and
I must start letting him go.*

I realize this verse has significant meaning for Zack also. My hope is he will be reminded to be on guard at all times- for everything from peer pressure to driving on the road. My hope is that this verse will give him encouragement as he navigates the road of life. He can be bold in his faith in God and draw strength from Him.

Perhaps you need encouragement today, too Have confidence that God is with you in whatever circumstance befalls you. He desires to be a very present part of every tiny detail of your life. Find peace in knowing that you can call on God anytime and He is there. Hopefully you will find strength in knowing that God is forevermore guiding you in standing firm in your faith.

I may be referring back to this scripture quite often as the driving lessons continue. I am blessed that I can rely on God to help me in those trying times - even when my son wants to be a race car driver.

Your thoughts:

_____

_____

_____

_____

_____

_____

~Fifty~

Waiting on the Moth

The Lord is good to those who wait for him, to the soul who seeks him. Lamentations 3:25 ESV

"Abby, come to the garage...quickly." I knew she would be so excited to see the chunky caterpillar crawling on the floor. As predicted, she was thrilled by my discovery and wanted to keep him. Minutes later, our little friend had a new home in a plastic container filled with grass and leaves.

Abby awoke early the next day to check on the critter. Surprised, she saw that the caterpillar had incased himself in a cocoon in the top corner of the plastic box. We were so excited because we knew it would only be a matter of time until a beautiful moth would emerge from the cocoon. It is so fascinating to watch God at work in the life cycle of insects and how He transforms them into new beings.

Now, my daughter and I are waiting. And waiting... And waiting... We check the plastic container several times a day to investigate for signs of change in the cocoon. Sadly, the encasement is dormant, no activity has been detected. It is hard for us to be patient and continue to wait. We are ready to see the beautiful designs on the wings of this new creature.

The moth has reminded me that sometimes in life, I must learn to be still and wait on God. Many times, I pray diligently for specific areas of my life and I sense God telling me to wait...wait on Him for His perfect timing. I have faith God has good things in store for me. I'm reassured God will help me grow and mature, just like the moth is growing and maturing right now in its cocoon. I need to pursue an attitude of forbearance and wait on the perfect timing of my Savior, for He knows what is best for me.

Maybe you have a "moth" that you are waiting on in your own life. Do not lose hope. Waiting is rarely ever easy. But find hope in reflecting on what the moth begins as and then to the wonderful transformation that entails. God wants to help us become beautiful beings in His sight. We just need to trust Him to complete the metamorphosis.

Your thoughts:

_____

_____

_____

_____

_____

_____

_____

_____

_____

_____

_____

_____

_____

_____

_____

_____

_____

_____

_____

~Fifty-One~

Power Walker

For we walk by faith, not by sight. 2 Corinthians 5:7

His hands were sweaty and his breathing quickened. Soon his knees began to tremble and he grasped the walker tighter. My patient's posture became stooped as he said, "I can't do this today. I cannot walk. I am not ready yet."

We had been working on building up standing tolerance for quite some time. Three times a week, I visited my patient to help him get stronger. Most days we worked on exercises and stood bedside with his rolling walker to help increase his endurance for walking.

Unfortunately, I don't think my patient has a future in power walking any time soon. His muscles are stronger but his faith is weak. The fear of falling prohibits the feet from moving forward, even just a little bit. He is completely paralyzed by fear and stuck in place. He lacks faith in himself as he doesn't feel capable of completing this physical task, even with me there to help him.

My patient and I have a lot in common. Many times I have been "stuck" in place, afraid to take that first step. Whether it is to take the leap of faith to start a new job or to have the courage to submit my writing to a magazine, voices in my head threaten my confidence and faith in myself and God.

When those voices are the loudest, I cling the hardest to God's promises in the Bible, especially the key verse from 2 Corinthians. Scripture encourages me to remember that even when I am weak, my faith in God is strong. Even when the desired outcome is not visible, when I cannot see how everything is going to work out, God does. He has my best interests at heart and has created and chosen me for a specific purpose. He gives me everything I need to fulfill that purpose as He equips the chosen, not chooses the equipped.

What is God asking you to do today? Have courage and faith to take the first steps toward that in which God is calling you to do. He will guide your steps and help you along the way. He will equip you with everything you need for success at following His will. Don't be stuck in place any longer-God has given you the ability to be a power walker.

Heavenly Father, thank you for loving me and choosing me for Your special purposes. Give me courage and perseverance to move forward in Your plan for my life. When Satan tries to persuade me I am not good enough, remind me of Your faithful love and promises that I am enough for You, as Your beloved child. In Jesus' name I pray, Amen."

Your thoughts:

_____

_____

_____

_____

_____

_____

_____

~Fifty-Two~

Identity Thief

Yet to all who have received Him, to those who believed in His name, He gave the right to become children of God. John 1:12 NIV

Have you ever felt invisible? That's exactly how I have felt for most of my life. Not that I haven't been loved and nurtured all along the way- it's just that I've never felt in touch with my true identity, the real Alisha Ritchie—until just recently, anyway. For as long as I can remember, I have always been known as my parents' youngest daughter or my siblings' younger sister. Now I have graduated to being referred to as Brandon's wife and Zack and Abby's mom. Even in church, I feel that I am known as the deacon's wife. While I enjoy being each one of those titles, I question myself, "Who exactly is Alisha Ritchie?" Surely there is more to me than those titles I carry? It's as if each label blurs and robs me of the reality of who I am truly created to be.

After being asked recently to give my testimony in a small group Bible study, the Lord pierced my heart with the realization my authentic identity is in Him. The Scriptures give me clues hinting to my genuine identification. I am fearfully and wonderfully made. I am a masterpiece created in the image of God. I am never alone. I can approach God with confidence and bring glory to Him. I am forgiven even though I do not deserve His grace. I am a light to others. I am chosen and dearly loved. All of these qualities point to the same real truth of my identity- I am adopted as a child of God, the one true King. In John, we read, "Yet to all who received him, to those who believed in his name, he gave the right to become children of God-." No title I have ever held in the past nor in the future can compare to the most precious one of being adopted into God's family. Knowing who I honestly am gives me new confidence to resolve I am not invisible. God gives me purpose to be seen and heard by sharing His story through inspirational writing.

Do you have assurance of your true identity? Trust in God to show you just how special you are to Him. Make a commitment to share your story with others so that your Father may be glorified. Pray for protection so that the titles you hold in your own life will not be a thief to the true purpose God has given you. Now when I think of myself and the legacy I hope to leave, I aspire my life evidences exactly who Alisha Ritchie is-an adopted daughter of the Most High God.

Your thoughts:

_____

_____

_____

_____

_____

_____

_____

_____

_____

_____

_____

_____

_____

_____

_____

_____

Snuggle Sessions with God   Alisha Ritchie

43535389R00064

Made in the USA
Middletown, DE
11 May 2017